THE JPS B'NAI MITZVAH TORAH COMMENTARY

Bo' (Exodus 10:1–13:16)
Haftarah (Jeremiah 46:13–28)

Rabbi Jeffrey K. Salkin

The Jewish Publication Society · Philadelphia
University of Nebraska Press · Lincoln

INTRODUCTION

News flash: the most important thing about becoming bar or bat mitzvah isn't the party. Nor is it the presents. Nor even being able to celebrate with your family and friends—as wonderful as those things are. Nor is it even standing before the congregation and reading the prayers of the liturgy—as important as that is.

No, the most important thing about becoming bar or bat mitzvah is sharing Torah with the congregation. And why is that? Because of all Jewish skills, that is the most important one.

Here is what is true about rites of passage: you can tell what a culture values by the tasks it asks its young people to perform on their way to maturity. In American culture, you become responsible for driving, responsible for voting, and yes, responsible for drinking responsibly.

In some cultures, the rite of passage toward maturity includes some kind of trial, or a test of strength. Sometimes, it is a kind of "outward bound" camping adventure. Among the Maasai tribe in Africa, it is traditional for a young person to hunt and kill a lion. In some Hispanic cultures, fifteen year-old girls celebrate the *quinceañera*, which marks their entrance into maturity.

What is Judaism's way of marking maturity? It combines both of these rites of passage: *responsibility* and *test*. You show that you are on your way to becoming a *responsible* Jewish adult through a public *test* of strength and knowledge—reading or chanting Torah, and then teaching it to the congregation.

This is the most important Jewish ritual mitzvah (commandment), and that is how you demonstrate that you are, truly, bar or bat mitzvah—old enough to be responsible for the mitzvot.

What Is Torah?

So, what exactly is the Torah? You probably know this already, but let's review.

The Torah (teaching) consists of "the five books of Moses," sometimes also called the *chumash* (from the Hebrew word *chameish*, which means "five"), or, sometimes, the Greek word Pentateuch (which means "the five teachings").

Here are the five books of the Torah, with their common names and their Hebrew names.

> **Genesis (The beginning), which in Hebrew is Bere'shit (from the first words—"When God began to create").** Bere'shit spans the years from Creation to Joseph's death in Egypt. Many of the Bible's best stories are in Genesis: the creation story itself; Adam and Eve in the Garden of Eden; Cain and Abel; Noah and the Flood; and the tales of the Patriarchs and Matriarchs, Abraham, Isaac, Jacob, Sarah, Rebekah, Rachel, and Leah. It also includes one of the greatest pieces of world literature, the story of Joseph, which is actually the oldest complete novel in history, comprising more than one-quarter of all Genesis.

> **Exodus (Getting out), which in Hebrew is Shemot (These are the names).** Exodus begins with the story of the Israelite slavery in Egypt. It then moves to the rise of Moses as a leader, and the Israelites' liberation from slavery. After the Israelites leave Egypt, they experience the miracle of the parting of the Sea of Reeds (or "Red Sea"); the giving of the Ten Commandments at Mount Sinai; the idolatry of the Golden Calf; and the design and construction of the Tabernacle and of the ark for the original tablets of the law, which our ancestors carried with them in the desert. Exodus also includes various ethical and civil laws, such as "You shall not wrong a stranger or oppress him, for you were strangers in the land of Egypt" (22:20).

> **Leviticus (about the Levites), or, in Hebrew, Va-yikra' (And God called).** It goes into great detail about the kinds of sacrifices that the ancient Israelites brought as offerings; the laws of ritual purity; the animals that were permitted and forbidden for eating (the beginnings of the tradition of kashrut, the Jewish dietary laws); the diagnosis of various skin diseases; the ethical laws of holiness; the ritual calendar of the Jewish year; and various agricultural laws concerning the treatment of the Land of Israel. Leviticus is basically the manual of ancient Judaism.

> Numbers (because the book begins with the census of the Israelites), or, in Hebrew, Be-midbar (In the wilderness). The book describes the forty years of wandering in the wilderness and the various rebellions against Moses. The constant theme: "Egypt wasn't so bad. Maybe we should go back." The greatest rebellion against Moses was the negative reports of the spies about the Land of Israel, which discouraged the Israelites from wanting to move forward into the land. For that reason, the "wilderness generation" must die off before a new generation can come into maturity and finish the journey.

> Deuteronomy (The repetition of the laws of the Torah), or, in Hebrew, Devarim (The words). The final book of the Torah is, essentially, Moses's farewell address to the Israelites as they prepare to enter the Land of Israel. Here we find various laws that had been previously taught, though sometimes with different wording. Much of Deuteronomy contains laws that will be important to the Israelites as they enter the Land of Israel—laws concerning the establishment of a monarchy and the ethics of warfare. Perhaps the most famous passage from Deuteronomy contains the *Shema*, the declaration of God's unity and uniqueness, and the *Ve-ahavta*, which follows it. Deuteronomy ends with the death of Moses on Mount Nebo as he looks across the Jordan Valley into the land that he will not enter.

Jews read the Torah in sequence—starting with Bere'shit right after Simchat Torah in the autumn, and then finishing Devarim on the following Simchat Torah. Each Torah portion is called a parashah (division; sometimes called a *sidrah*, a place in the order of the Torah reading). The stories go around in a full circle, reminding us that we can always gain more insights and more wisdom from the Torah. This means that if you don't "get" the meaning this year, don't worry—it will come around again.

And What Else? The Haftarah

We read or chant the Torah from the Torah scroll—the most sacred thing that a Jewish community has in its possession. The Torah is written without vowels, and the ability to read it and chant it is part of the challenge and the test.

But there is more to the synagogue reading. Every Torah reading has an accompanying haftarah reading. Haftarah means "conclusion," because there was once a time when the service actually ended with that reading. Some scholars believe that the reading of the haftarah originated at a time when non-Jewish authorities outlawed the reading of the Torah, and the Jews read the haftarah sections instead. In fact, in some synagogues, young people who become bar or bat mitzvah read very little Torah and instead read the entire haftarah portion.

The haftarah portion comes from the Nevi'im, the prophetic books, which are the second part of the Jewish Bible. It is either read or chanted from a Hebrew Bible, or maybe from a booklet or a photocopy.

The ancient sages chose the haftarah passages because their themes reminded them of the words or stories in the Torah text. Sometimes, they chose *haftarah* with special themes in honor of a festival or an upcoming festival.

Not all books in the prophetic section of the Hebrew Bible consist of prophecy. Several are historical. For example:

The book of Joshua tells the story of the conquest and settlement of Israel.

The book of Judges speaks of the period of early tribal rulers who would rise to power, usually for the purpose of uniting the tribes in war against their enemies. Some of these leaders are famous: Deborah, the great prophetess and military leader, and Samson, the biblical strong man.

The books of Samuel start with Samuel, the last judge, and then move to the creation of the Israelite monarchy under Saul and David (approximately 1000 BCE).

The books of Kings tell of the death of King David, the rise of King Solomon, and how the Israelite kingdom split into the Northern Kingdom of Israel and the Southern Kingdom of Judah (approximately 900 BCE).

And then there are the books of the prophets, those spokesmen for God whose words fired the Jewish conscience. Their names are immortal: Isaiah, Jeremiah, Ezekiel, Amos, Hosea, among others.

Someone once said: "There is no evidence of a biblical prophet ever being invited back a second time for dinner." Why? Because the prophets were tough. They had no patience for injustice, apathy, or hypocrisy. No one escaped their criticisms. Here's what they taught:

> God commands the Jews to behave decently toward one another. In fact, God cares more about basic ethics and decency than about ritual behavior.
> God chose the Jews *not* for special privileges, but for special duties to humanity.
> As bad as the Jews sometimes were, there was always the possibility that they would improve their behavior.
> As bad as things might be now, it will not always be that way. Someday, there will be universal justice and peace. Human history is moving forward toward an ultimate conclusion that some call the Messianic Age: a time of universal peace and prosperity for the Jewish people and for all the people of the world.

Your Mission—To Teach Torah to the Congregation

On the day when you become bar or bat mitzvah, you will be reading, or chanting, Torah—in Hebrew. You will be reading, or chanting, the haftarah—in Hebrew. That is the major skill that publicly marks the becoming of bar or bat mitzvah. But, perhaps even more important than that, you need to be able to teach something about the Torah portion, and perhaps the haftarah as well.

And that is where this book comes in. It will be a very valuable resource for you, and your family, in the b'nai mitzvah process.

Here is what you will find in it:

> A brief **summary** of every Torah portion. This is a basic overview of the portion; and, while it might not refer to everything in the Torah portion, it will explain its most important aspects.
> A list of the **major ideas** in the Torah portion. The purpose: to make the Torah portion real, in ways that we can relate to. Every Torah portion contains unique ideas, and when you put all

of those ideas together, you actually come up with a list of Judaism's most important ideas.

> Two ***divrei Torah*** ("words of Torah," or "sermonettes") for each portion. These *divrei Torah* explain significant aspects of the Torah portion in accessible, reader-friendly language. Each *devar Torah* contains references to **traditional** Jewish sources (those that were written before the modern era), as well as **modern** sources and quotes. We have searched, far and wide, to find sources that are unusual, interesting, and not just the "same old stuff" that many people already know about the Torah portion. Why did we include these minisermons in the volume? Not because we want you to simply copy those sermons and pass them off as your own (that would be cheating), though you are free to quote from them. We included them so that you can see what is possible— how you can try to make meaning for yourself out of the words of Torah.

> **Connections:** This is perhaps the most valuable part. It's a list of questions that you can ask yourself, or that others might help you think about—any of which can lead to the creation of your *devar Torah.*

Note: you don't have to like everything that's in a particular Torah portion. Some aren't that loveable. Some are hard to understand; some are about religious practices that people today might find confusing, and even offensive; some contain ideas that we might find totally outmoded.

But this doesn't have to get in the way. After all, most kids spend a lot of time thinking about stories that contain ideas that modern people would find totally bizarre. Any good medieval fantasy story falls into that category.

And we also believe that, if you spend just a little bit of time with those texts, you can begin to understand what the author was trying to say.

This volume goes one step further. Sometimes, the haftarah comes off as a second thought, and no one really thinks about it. We have tried to solve that problem by including a **summary** of each haftarah, and then a mini-sermon on the haftarah. This will help you learn how these sacred words are relevant to today's world, and even to your own life.

All Bible quotations come from the NJPS translation, which is found in the many different editions of the JPS TANAKH; in the Conservative movement's *Etz Hayim: Torah and Commentary;* in the Reform movement's *Torah: A Modern Commentary;* and in other Bible commentaries and study guides.

How Do I Write a *Devar Torah?*

It really is easier than it looks.

There are many ways of thinking about the *devar Torah*. It is, of course, a short sermon on the meaning of the Torah (and, perhaps, the haftarah) portion. It might even be helpful to think of the *devar Torah* as a "book report" on the portion itself.

The most important thing you can know about this sacred task is: *Learn* the words. *Love* the words. Teach people what it could mean to *live* the words.

Here's a basic outline for a *devar Torah:*

"My Torah portion is (name of portion)_____,
    from the book of _____, chapter

_____.
"In my Torah portion, we learn that_____
    (Summary of portion)
"For me, the most important lesson of this Torah portion is (what
    is the best thing in the portion? Take the portion as a whole;
    your *devar Torah* does not have to be only, or specifically, on the
    verses that you are reading).
"As I learned my Torah portion, I found myself wondering:
    ➤ *Raise a question that the Torah portion itself raises.*
    ➤ *"Pick a fight"* with the portion. Argue with it.
    ➤ *Answer a question* that is listed in the "Connections" section of
        each Torah portion.
    ➤ *Suggest a question to your rabbi* that you would want the rabbi
        to answer in his or her own *devar Torah* or sermon.

"I have lived the values of the Torah by _____
(here, you can talk about how the Torah portion relates to your
own life. If you have done a mitzvah project, you can talk about
that here).

How To Keep It from Being Boring
(and You from Being Bored)

Some people just don't like giving traditional speeches. From our per-
spective, that's really okay. Perhaps you can teach Torah in a different
way—one that makes sense to you.

> Write an "open letter" to one of the characters in your Torah por-
  tion. "Dear Abraham: I hope that your trip to Canaan was not too
  hard . . ." "Dear Moses: Were you afraid when you got the Ten
  Commandments on Mount Sinai? I sure would have been . . ."
> Write a news story about what happens. Imagine yourself to
  be a television or news reporter. "Residents of neighboring cities were horrified yesterday as the wicked cities of Sodom and
  Gomorrah were burned to the ground. Some say that God was
  responsible . . ."
> Write an imaginary interview with a character in your Torah portion.
> Tell the story from the point of view of another character, or a mi-
  nor character, in the story. For instance, tell the story of the Gar-
  den of Eden from the point of view of the serpent. Or the story
  of the Binding of Isaac from the point of view of the ram, which
  was substituted for Isaac as a sacrifice. Or perhaps the story of
  the sale of Joseph from the point of view of his coat, which was
  stripped off him and dipped in a goat's blood.
> Write a poem about your Torah portion.
> Write a song about your Torah portion.
> Write a play about your Torah portion, and have some friends act
  it out with you.
> Create a piece of artwork about your Torah portion.

The bottom line is: Make this a joyful experience. Yes—it could
even be fun.

The Very Last Thing You Need to Know at This Point

The Torah scroll is written without vowels. Why? Don't *sofrim* (Torah scribes) know the vowels?

Of course they do.

So, why do they leave the vowels out?

One reason is that the Torah came into existence at a time when sages were still arguing about the proper vowels, and the proper pronunciation.

But here is another reason: The Torah text, as we have it today, and as it sits in the scroll, is actually *an unfinished work*. Think of it: the words are just sitting there. Because they have no vowels, it is as if they have no voice.

When we read the Torah publicly, we give voice to the ancient words. And when we find meaning in those ancient words, and we talk about those meanings, those words jump to life. They enter our lives. They make our world deeper and better.

Mazal tov to you, and your family. This is your journey toward Jewish maturity. Love it.

THE TORAH

❖ Bo': Exodus 10:1–13:16

No doubt about it, Pharaoh has a problem. He has got to be one of the slowest learners in all of world history. Because Pharaoh's heart continues to be hardened, and because his stubbornness persists, God continues to bring plagues upon Egypt. This portion features the plagues of locusts, darkness, and, the worst of them all, the death of the firstborn. At that point, Pharaoh finally relents and lets the Israelites go.

God tells Moses and Aaron that they will depart from Egypt in the first month, and that on the tenth day of that month each Israelite household should acquire a lamb. At twilight on the fourteenth day, each household should slaughter their lamb, putting some of its blood on the doorposts so that their houses are spared the plague of the death of the firstborn. The Israelites must also eat unleavened bread (matzah) for seven days.

These observances—the sacrifice of the lamb and the eating of matzah—will become important parts of the festival of Pesach. The Israelites are further told to consecrate their firstborn to God, as a further remembrance of their departure from Egypt.

Summary

➤ Pharaoh still stubbornly refuses to let the Israelites go. The final plagues of locusts, darkness, and the death of the firstborn come upon the Egyptians. (10:12–11:10)

➤ God commands Moses to establish the festival of Pesach. (12:1–23)

➤ The Israelites are commanded to tell their children about the meaning of Pesach—which means telling them about the meaning of freedom itself. (12:24–27)

➤ God gives Moses the laws of the Pesach sacrifice. (12:43–49)

The Big Ideas

> **Jews must be a distinct people.** That is why the final act of liberation for the Israelites is to sacrifice a lamb. The lamb was one of Egypt's most important gods. Publicly slaughtering the lamb was how the Israelites would declare that they did not worship that god, and, by doing that, the Israelites had no choice but to leave Egypt.

> **Rituals help us remember important ideas and keep them alive.** Rituals help us feel that we, personally, are part of Jewish history. Whether or not the biblical account of the Exodus is historically accurate, when we remember it we relearn moral lessons that have shaped human history.

> **Education is one of Judaism's most important values.** It guarantees that Judaism will be passed down through the generations. Asking questions, as we do at the Passover seder, is the most important part of learning.

> **When we celebrate, we must remember those who are poor or are without family.** That is why the Torah commands Jews to join together with other families that cannot afford their own lamb for the Pesach sacrifice. Even though we do not sacrifice animals anymore, all our celebrations should remind us that there is a world beyond ourselves.

Divrei Torah

WHY DO YOU HAVE TO KILL THE EGYPTIAN GOD?

As many scholars have noted, the plagues that struck Egypt during the Exodus can be interpreted as being assaults on the various gods of Egypt: the Nile, the sun, even to the firstborn of Pharaoh. But after the "official" plagues have ended, one more Egyptian god will come under assault. "Speak to the whole community of Israel and say that on the tenth of this month [the first month, Nisan] each of them shall take a lamb to a family, a lamb to a household" (12:3). God told the Israelites to acquire a *lamb*—which is not just an animal, but an Egyptian animal god.

In other words, it seems as if God is telling the Israelites to get themselves an Egyptian lamb-god and therefore buy into the Egyptian religious system—which means becoming good Egyptians.

The Israelites must live with their lamb-gods for four days. That's enough time to become comfortable with their new gods. It is also enough time for their Egyptian neighbors to have seen them with their new gods and to have therefore assumed that the Israelites are (finally) prepared to fit into Egyptian life and to stop being outsiders.

Not so fast.

The Israelites then slaughter their lambs. They dab the blood on the doorposts of their houses—in a place where everyone can see it. That is why a midrash portrays God as understanding that "as long as the Israelites worship the Egyptian gods, they shall not be redeemed. Withdraw your hands from idolatry and take a lamb, and therefore slaughter the gods of Egypt and make the Passover."

The slaughtering of the lambs, therefore, did not only symbolize physical freedom and national redemption. It was also an outward manifestation of freedom from Egyptian idolatry—and, with that, the Israelites are ready to truly make their break with Egypt. As Rabbi Lawrence Kushner has written about the ill-fated lamb: "Come tomorrow and its blood is on our door, we leave with Moses, or they will surely kill us. A slave who can kill the master's god is no longer a slave. And if we are afraid to kill the lamb, then we may not leave with Moses."

Today, killing lambs (especially since they are no longer worshiped as gods) is not our idea of a good time, nor is it a symbolic act. But when our ancestors made their courageous break for freedom they had to break with every aspect of their enslavement. This has always been one of the great things about the Jews: the willingness to stand apart and to be different. Why? To make a better world.

DID THE EXODUS REALLY HAPPEN?
DOES IT MATTER?

One of the most famous composers in American history was George Gershwin. He was also Jewish. In one of his most famous songs, we find the words: "The stuff that you're liable to find in the Bible, they ain't necessarily so." Gershwin had a good sense of humor. The melody of "It Ain't Necessarily So" sounds very similar to the traditional Torah blessing!

So is it "necessarily so" that the Israelites went forth from Egypt? Did the Exodus really happen? Well, as the song says, not necessarily.

First, the Torah says that six hundred thousand men (not counting the women and the children) left Egypt and then wandered across the Sinai Desert to get to the Land of Israel. But archeologists have not found a trace of evidence that anyone was ever there! And, if you put together all those who supposedly came out of Egypt, they would have created a long line of people that would have stretched all the way from Egypt to Israel!

What about in the Land of Israel itself? Here, again, archeologists tell us that there is no evidence for a huge group of people entering the Land of Israel at that time. If that had been the case, then, at the very least, there would have been a sudden, vast increase in the amount of pottery that was made, but archeologists have found no evidence for increased amounts of pottery. So, the general opinion among archeologists and historians is that while there were some Israelite slaves who left Egypt, most Israelites lived in the Land of Israel for many generations. They never left and they never had to return.

On the other hand: what nation would ever invent a history of itself that says that it started out in slavery? In the words of modern scholar Eli Barnavi: "It is highly improbable that a nation would choose to invent for itself a history of slavery as an explanation for its origins." And, as an old saying goes, "The absence of evidence is not evidence of absence." A group of nomads, even a large one, could have traveled across the great desert and, after these thousands of years, hardly left a trace.

The Torah is probably not one hundred percent historically accurate. But does that really matter? Whether or not it happened just the way that the Torah says, the Exodus from Egypt teaches us about the value of human freedom and of human hope. And not just for Jews. "In every generation, a person [not: "a Jew"] should see himself or herself as if he or she had personally gone forth from Egypt, states the Passover Haggadah.

We are probably not going to come to a definitive answer to the question "Did the Exodus really happen?" That's all right. We can live with not knowing for sure. No matter what the archeologists and historians finally conclude, the Exodus is part of our heritage and how we view our origins and character. The Exodus, our journey from slavery to freedom, politically and spiritually, didn't just happen once in history. It happens within each of us. And it happens all the time.

Connections

> Do you believe that the plagues were necessary in order for the Israelites to be able to leave Egypt? What alternatives could have been possible?
> What are the most important questions that you have about Judaism, or about life?
> How has Jewish education been important to you and your family?
> What kind of Pesach memories does your family have? Has it been a memorable holiday for you and your family? What does it mean to you?
> Do you believe that the Exodus really happened? Do you think that it matters if it did or not? In what way have you personally felt that you have gone out of Egypt? What is your Egypt? (For example, breaking a bad habit, overcoming a difficulty at school, etc.)

THE HAFTARAH

❖ Bo': Jeremiah 46:13–28

Pharaoh just doesn't get it, whether it was the Pharaoh who lived in the time of Moses, or the Pharaoh who lived in the time of Jeremiah. The later Pharaoh has a starring role in this haftarah. In this week's Torah portion the earlier Pharaoh cannot make the right decisions, and here the later Pharaoh has the same problem.

The prophet Jeremiah who (like Ezekiel) preached in the time before the Babylonians destroyed the kingdom of Judah, counsels the Judeans not to make an alliance with Egypt against Babylon. He's concerned about his fellow Judeans' flight to Egypt. It won't work, he says. He predicts that the Egyptians will be unstable allies, and that their kingdom—like the regime of the Pharaoh of Moses's time—will fall to ruin.

Jerk Alert, Part Two

In last week's haftarah, the prophet Ezekiel warned the Judeans that it was no use trying to make an alliance with the Egyptians. This week, the prophet Jeremiah is saying pretty much the same thing about the Pharaoh of his time.

The Pharaoh who rules during Moses's time was totally arrogant because he thought that he was divine—that he had actually created the Nile for himself. And, this week, we see another symptom of Pharaoh's inability to get it. Jeremiah calls the Pharaoh of his time a "braggart who let the hour go by" (46:17). Actually, "braggart" is only an approximate translation of the Hebrew word *sha'on*. Rashi, the great medieval commentator, teaches: "Pharaoh was a big noise-maker who raised his voice." He was the loudmouth who never shut up. Pharaoh was, as they say, all hot air—a really big disappointment as a leader.

This should not surprise us. Go back to the Pharaoh of Moses's time. First, God hardened his heart and made him refuse to let the Israelites go, thus bringing on more and more plagues, each one worse than the last. It is as if Pharaoh encounters each plague as the first one. It is as if he has no memory of what has already happened to his land and to his people. More than that, he is so convinced of his own power—after all, he thinks he is a god—that he just lets the time slip away from him. He thinks that he has all the time in the world—and then, Egypt falls apart. That is the way it is with the Pharaoh of Jeremiah's time as well. In the process, they hurt not just themselves, but everyone and everything around them.

You probably know people like Pharaoh. There is always that kid who thinks she is so great—such a great athlete, such a great student—that she gets lazy. Sure, she brags a lot. But while she brags she wastes time that she could have devoted to becoming even better. She misses crucial opportunities. She is the "braggart who let the hour go by."

But there is something else going on here as well. Jeremiah knows something that all the Egyptians and the Judeans should have known as well. "Been there, done that." The Israelites had a bad experience with Egypt and Pharaoh (to put it mildly). They should know better than to think that Egypt is all-powerful. Back in the days of Moses, the plagues were a way of fighting the power of the Egyptian gods. That same battle is going on in the haftarah portion: "The Lord of Hosts, the God of Israel, has said: I will inflict punishment on Amon of No and on Pharaoh—on Egypt, her gods, and her kings" (46:25). And the Egyptians themselves should have learned from their historical experience. But they didn't.

When it comes to the Jews, nations don't learn their lessons. Nations that have oppressed the Jews, from ancient Egypt to medieval England and Spain, have come to regret it. Sir Winston Churchill expressed this in strong terms: "Some people like Jews and some do not, but no thoughtful man can doubt the fact that they are beyond all question the most formidable and the most remarkable race which has ever appeared in the world."

Nations and peoples need to stay humble, guard against arrogance, and guard against the tendency to belittle others and become aloof and cruel. Nobody wants to be a jerk, but it can happen. And that can be dangerous for your country, your community, and yourself.

❖ Notes

❖ Notes

CPSIA information can be obtained
at www.ICGtesting.com
Printed in the USA
LVHW08s0951050818
585984LV00004B/425/P